I Hate Writing Papers, but I Want an "A"

EILEEN PUECHNER

I Hate Writing Papers, but I Want an "A"

TATE PUBLISHING & *Enterprises*

Tate Publishing is committed to excellence in the publishing industry. Our staff of highly trained professionals, including editors, graphic designers, and marketing personnel, work together to produce the very finest books available. The company reflects the philosophy established by the founders, based on Psalms 68:11,

"THE LORD GAVE THE WORD AND GREAT WAS THE COMPANY OF THOSE WHO PUBLISHED IT."

If you would like further information, please contact us:
1.888.361.9473 | www.tatepublishing.com
TATE PUBLISHING & *Enterprises*, LLC | 127 E. Trade Center Terrace
Mustang, Oklahoma 73064 USA

I Hate Writing Papers but I Want an "A"
Cover design by Lynly Taylor
Interior design by Sarah Leis

Published in the United States of America
ISBN: 978–1-6024716–6-5
07.03.05

ACKNOWLEDGEMENTS

This book would not have been possible without the constant prodding of my husband, Marc. It was his idea to create this book, and he refused to take no for an answer when I hesitated to write it. Thanks for hanging in there with me and providing invaluable insight into the minds of the non-English majors of the world. I love you!

Many thanks and much love to my family for insisting for years that I try writing as a career. Yes, you all told me so. Thank you for cheering me on and reviewing my work.

To all my friends who read this little book and offered their input and encouragement, thank you all. I won't list all your names because I'll forget someone and the omission will torture me.

Of course, without the belief of the Acquisitions Editor, Janey Hayes, at Tate Publishing, this book wouldn't exist at all. Thank you for starting me on this path. I hope to justify your faith in me. Undying thanks to Kylie Lyons, my editor, for her astute comments and to Lynly Taylor, my graphic artist, for her amazing cover.

Most importantly, I give God the credit and thanks for getting me here. May I use this talent in a way that glorifies You.

TABLE OF CONTENTS

FOREWORD

I know what you're thinking: can a book this small really help me get an "A"? The answer is yes if you are willing to put the time and effort into your work. Any great inventor, artist, hall of fame rock group, and sports team dynasty have committed time and effort to achieve their status.

If you're like me, doing the research or knowing what you want to write about is relatively easy. The hard part is putting your ideas on paper in a manner that makes sense to the general reader and makes an impression on your instructor. During high school and as an undergrad, I spent many hours writing with nothing better than a "B+" to show for it. When I started grad school, the idea of writing many papers made me very nervous. In graduate work, professors hold you to a higher standard. You can't just pass; a "C" is not acceptable. So, knowing my track record with composing essays, my confidence was rather low. Thankfully, God blessed me with my wife, Eileen, who was willing to look at my work and give me a few pointers. Not only was Eileen an English major, but her father was also a high school English teacher, so she grew up in a very articulate environment. The result of those tips was an "A-" or better on every paper I wrote and the inspiration for this book.

I felt strongly that Eileen needed to compile these teachings in a form that was easy to read and understandable. The problem with most books on grammar or writing is that the author speaks in a language or uses terminology that confuses the average student. This book keeps it simple.

Your paper is like a meal in a fine restaurant. A chef may cook a delicious dinner, but it's the presentation of the food that actually enhances the flavor of what you're eating. Not only does the meal taste scrumptious and smell enticing, the brain also registers the visual pleasure, which increases the enjoyment of the experience. This book helps you learn how to take your writing to the next level by taking your good content and arranging it attractively so your instructor will enjoy it. I used these concepts of scholastic writing, and they worked for me. If you're willing to put in the time and effort, you will achieve top grades too.

Marc Puechner
M.A. in Religious Studies

INTRODUCTION

The Inspiration to Write This Book

I wrote this book because my husband, Marc, insisted I should. It all started when he began graduate school. He'd graduated from college ten years before and asked me, a former English major, to look over his papers. I found several grammatical issues in his work, and when I tried to explain the rules to him, I failed to convey the information in a way he could comprehend. I understood why his style was problematic, so why didn't he get it? I had to put the guidelines into a less intimidating form that made sense to him.

Marc also had another bad habit: he tried to write and edit his research work at the same time. When I first told him that he needed to spend more time revising and proofreading his papers after the rough draft stage, he didn't know what the big deal was. I was frustrated trying to explain it to him until I compared writing to making music. As a singer and electric bass player, he could see the benefit of spending many hours working out a song's lyrics or a complicated bass line; when I likened the often difficult experience of writing to that kind of musical struggle, he finally understood.

The results were immediate and positive. My husband never received a grade below an A- throughout his studies. He thought that incorporating the various points that I'd taught him into a grammar book would be very helpful to many students who, like him, didn't like grammar and didn't have the time or inclination to learn its intricacies.

Who needs this book?

I realize that a few people can throw together an "A" paper at the last minute, but they are in the minority. If you are in the vast majority and wish to create an impressive paper but don't have the patience to wade through a fat volume outlining every rule (or even a small publication that may be written for people who already seem to "get it"), then this book is for you.

This information applies to any student at any level who needs to write an essay or term paper. Whether you are a high school student or a post-graduate level professional, these basic guidelines will improve your work and earn you a better grade. I don't cover all the rules of grammar because I'm trying to keep things simple. Eventually, I hope you will pick up one of those "fat volumes" to study the finer points of the English language, but until then, this is a good place to start. Some of it may be oversimplified, but my intention is to help as many people as possible.

Why is this information important?

In graduate school, my husband's professors began each semester by handing out their criteria for grading, and every one of them listed good grammar as a point of emphasis. One professor even spent a good portion of one class venting his frustration about bad writing and poor grammar in student papers. Every issue that this instructor cited was a point that I had mentioned to Marc over the course of his three years of graduate work.

These rules are the backbone of good writing. It doesn't matter whether you're creating a paper for history, English, biology, or any other class. Any course that requires an essay or term paper will use the same criteria for a good grade. Perhaps your instructors won't mark the particular mistakes, but these are the points that they are looking for in a well-written paper. Different rules apply to the written word compared to the verbal form of the language. If you try to construct a paper the way you speak, you will not do well because the spoken language doesn't conform to grammar rules as stringently as the written form does.

How do you use it?

You must give yourself enough time to work through all the steps in this book.

A good portion of the writing process requires lengthy editing sessions. You will take less time as you become a stronger writer, but in the beginning, you will need an extensive period of time to edit and revise. Think of the difference between a microwave and an oven. The former doesn't need time to heat up and it works very quickly. The latter must preheat and then it cooks relatively slowly. Even though it takes a great deal longer, some foods taste much better if they're cooked in the oven. You can "microwave" your paper and try to finish it quickly, but it will only turn out well if you "bake it thoroughly in the oven." After researching extensively, don't cheat yourself out of a good grade just to finish the assignment.

I've outlined ten basic rules for good writing and then included several tables at the end of this book for reference. Read through the rules first to familiarize yourself with their content. Even experienced writers don't write "perfect" papers at the rough draft stage. Consult these tips periodically as you write until they become ingrained in your writing process. In addition, I have compiled, with explanations and examples of usage, many of the problematic phrases and words that people use incorrectly. If you are unsure about which version of a word belongs in your paper (for example, accept versus except), these tables will assist you.

I wish you success in your writing, and I promise that the process will get easier the more you use these guidelines.

1. GETTING YOUR IDEAS DOWN

Sometimes the worst part of writing a paper is just getting started. You're staring at an empty page or a blank screen, and you have no idea what to say. Don't worry if you don't have your subject fully developed before you begin writing. Just let your ideas flow. If you're someone who prefers to write on paper before typing it up, you might want to use every other line so you have space to change your mind. Give yourself permission to scratch out sections, write in the margins, use arrows, or leave notes to yourself. This kind of stream of consciousness writing will help you to create a formal (or informal) outline, as you develop the content of your paper. Edit the paper afterwards. If you become too concerned about how the paper sounds at the preliminary stage, you may lose your train of thought and never recall it. You will have an easier time reworking an existing paper than creating one from scratch. Many times, students make the mistake of trying to avoid a rough draft by trying to make their papers perfect on the first pass. As a result, their ideas seem sketchy, incoherent, and underdeveloped.

You can't possibly focus on every aspect of a paper all at once. You will need to walk away from your writing several times and then go back and look at it again to make sure that you've covered all the topics discussed in this book.

2. STRONG THESIS, INTRODUCTION, AND CLOSING PARAGRAPH

Do you ever have trouble staying on track with your topic? This is the section for you. Other than a blank page, one of the biggest obstacles to overcome is staying on topic. A good thesis and introduction will give direction to your whole work. A closing paragraph will sum up all the important points in your essay and remind the reader of your thesis. It's like tying up your subject in a bow.

Thesis

An "A" paper contains a strong, provable thesis. Your thesis statement is the last line of the introduction of your paper, and often it is one of the most important points you want to get across. Your thesis must be specific or you won't be able to focus your information into a concise whole; it'll be too long and too general. Think of your thesis as the hub of a wheel. If the hub is weak, the wheel will be too; if the thesis is weak, the paper will be as well. It often doesn't even matter if your thesis is "correct" (that is, that your instructor agrees with you) as long as you make a good case for your idea.

General
Shakespeare is a good writer.

Specific
Shakespeare introduced the most memorable and tragic characters in theater: Romeo and Juliet.

General
The Civil War hurt the South.

Specific
The Civil War temporarily ruined the South's economy and subjugated the South to the more industrial North.

General
The Web is a great invention.

Specific
The World Wide Web's influence secures its place as the most important invention in history.

Introduction

People often stumble right out of the blocks when writing a paper by trying to prove their entire position or explain all of their reasoning within the first paragraph. Bad idea. Keep your introduction short.

You'll have the opportunity to detail all your research in the body of your composition. By saying too much too early, you end up repeating yourself later, which weakens your work. It looks as though you're repeating yourself to fill up space. This paragraph should grab the reader's attention quickly and conclude with the thesis. It's like a movie preview, except that your paper is the coming attraction.

A good way to begin is with a quote. Perhaps you want to investigate books of literary criticism, famous sayings, or even pop culture references that fit your topic and then tie them into your intro.

Closing Paragraph

Once you've finished writing the rest of your piece, the closing paragraph should be a snap. Again, keep this paragraph short. In addition, this is not the place to introduce a new topic. If you have another subject that you wish to explore, add it to the body of the paper. You've already spent the time explaining your argument, so you don't need to start another in-depth discussion at the end. As I mentioned in "Introduction," by repeating yourself at length in your conclusion, you appear to be just filling up space, which weakens the paper. Briefly revisit the main points of your work and restate the thesis. There should be a sense of finality to your work such that you don't need more information to convey your point.

3. SUPPORTING PARAGRAPHS WITH GOOD TOPIC SENTENCES

So now that you have the attention of your reader, how do you keep it? If your thesis is the hub of a wheel, your supporting points are the spokes that extend from it.

In an "A" paper, each paragraph must begin with a sentence that supports the thesis and then has at least two additional points to support it. In an outline, you can't have a point A without a point B. The same is true of a supporting paragraph. All the paragraphs in the paper need to back up your thesis. If they do, your paper will never wander off course. You need to have examples to back up your argument. If you can't think of at least two statements that support the topic sentence, scrap that paragraph and start over; it's not important enough to include in your paper. You must clearly and logically develop your ideas in an organized form.

People often write a thesis and then compare it to their supporting paragraphs rather than the other way around; as a result, the thesis statement keeps changing. Pick an argument and stick to it; otherwise, your paper will lose focus and strength. Keep rereading your thesis statement to make sure that your writing continues to support your main idea.

You can see that if you haven't researched your idea, you'll have trouble compiling points to discuss. You must investigate your topic thoroughly and use adequate secondary sources to prove your thesis. Your instructors will always know if you're just dancing around an idea, trying to sound intelligent. Know what you're talking about or your grade will suffer.

4. POWERFUL VERBS

Individuals throughout history have used words to inspire and motivate the populace. Gandhi, Blessed Teresa of Calcutta, Martin Luther King Jr., and Adolf Hitler all used words to change the course of history; their words exuded power and emotion.

That's what you need to do in your work. I can't stress this point enough: "A" papers contain verbs with "punch." By punch, I mean a word that is descriptive.

> *For example:*
> She walked along the road.
>
> She meandered along the road.

In the first sentence, you know that the person was moving her feet; in the second sentence, you know she was lazily proceeding, taking her time. "Meandered" paints a vivid picture that "walked" doesn't portray, and you don't need to add any other words to express that activity.

Your word choice has a huge impact on the interest

your reader (your instructor or anyone else) will have and the grade you will earn. A strong verb will keep your statements short and to the point. Even though extra words will help you fulfill the page requirements of your paper, powerful verbs will improve your work. If you're worried about page length at this point, let's face it: you need to do more research.

The verb "to be" (am, are, is) often indicates a "weak" verb structure. "Weak" means you have to add more words to say what one powerful verb would to convey your thought. A weak verb structure also puts your sentence into the passive voice. If "the passive voice" is an unfamiliar term, hang in there. I'll describe all the details in "Passive Voice."

5. VARIED VOCABULARY

Remember those strong verbs that I just talked about? A wide vocabulary plays the same role in an "A" paper; it strengthens your paper and gives it "punch." For example, instead of boring your reader using the word "war" twenty-five times, use "conflict" or "battle."

Here's an example of how using the same verb repetitively drags down a paragraph:

> My two black Labrador Retrievers love playing. Each one plays a different game. Cosmo delights in playing fetch with his toys, whereas Conan prefers to play chase. They can play for hours.

Here's the same example using different expressions:

> My two black Labrador Retrievers love playing. Each one enjoys a different game. Cosmo delights in a round of fetch with his toys, whereas Conan prefers to engage in "chase me around the coffee table." They can amuse themselves for hours.

See how much more interesting it is to read a paragraph when you don't repeat the same word? *Note:* You may have to add or subtract a few words when you substitute terms from a thesaurus.

Here is another example of a boring paragraph in which a single noun ("clothing") is overused:

> Drew had a very messy bedroom. He left smelly clothes on his bed. Clothes hung from the lamp. He had piled dirty clothes in a darkened corner. Ragged clothes drooped from the top of his dresser and slipped unnoticed next to the wall. The only place he didn't have clothes was in his closet!

Fix the problem by using more specific and descriptive nouns:

> Drew had a very messy bedroom. He left smelly uniforms on his bed. Sweat suits hung from the lamp. He had piled dirty socks in a darkened corner. Ragged T-shirts drooped from the top of his dresser and slipped unnoticed next to the wall. The only place he didn't have clothes was in his closet!

Precise word choices show that you comprehend a subject because you can verbalize your thoughts in more than one way. On the other hand, a narrow vocabulary can bore and possibly confuse your instructor. To make sure you're using a variety of terms, make a thesaurus your best friend; find one and use it. It's set up like a dictionary, and it lists synonyms (words that have the same meaning). One word of caution: make sure you understand the meaning of a word before you use it. If you include a term just because it sounds clever without looking it up in the dictionary, you won't say what you think you're saying, and your attempt to sound brilliant will backfire. The following two examples demonstrate that situation.

Each of the following sentences contains a synonym for the word "actor" with definitions that are related but change the meaning of the examples:

> When the thespian fell ill, the production used an understudy until he recovered.

> When the impersonator fell ill, the production used an understudy until he recovered.

The first sentence uses an appropriate synonym, but the second uses a word that changes the idea. Sometimes the slight difference in nuance isn't a problem, but always check the dictionary to make sure the word conveys the meaning you intend.

Think of yourself as a painter who works with words

instead of paint. The more varied your word choice, the more "colors" you have to express your ideas. Along with thorough research, a thesaurus and dictionary are essential tools for creating an "A" paper.

6. CORRECT GRAMMAR AND PUNCTUATION

Yuck! Boring! Yes, I know that, at worst, you probably don't care about grammar or, at best, you don't understand all of its principles; however, you must have a basic grasp of grammar to earn an "A" paper. Although people tend to break the rules when they're speaking, instructors will not tolerate bad grammar in academic writing, and you will suffer the wrath of your teacher's red pen. Good punctuation directs a reader and helps that person understand the words on the page. Bad grammar frustrates and confuses a reader. Translation: low grade. Many books discuss the seemingly endless guidelines, but here are some basics:

Grammar and Puncuation

	Description	Example
Subject	*what or who* your sentence is about (noun—person, place, or thing)	My *friend* lives three hundred miles away. *(continued)*

Verb	the *action* your subject is taking	The frantic fans *fought* in line to get the last tickets to the soccer game.
Predicate	Verb plus words that complete the verb phrase	The frantic fans *fought in line to get the last tickets to the soccer game.* *fought* = verb *fought in line to get the last tickets to the soccer game* = predicate
Capitalization	Cap. all proper nouns (titles, names, places)	The *White House* is located in *Washington, D.C.* The *President* lives there.
Clause	*Independent*: a group of words that can stand on its own as a sentence *Dependent*: a group of words that cannot stand on its own as a sentence	Alyssa lives on this street. *Frank hurried to finish his exam* as the bell rang. On the way to school Next to the playground Walking on the beach *(continued)*

Commas	Use in a list of items.	Thomas Jefferson, John Adams, and Benjamin Franklin provided key leadership at the birth of the country.
	Use to separate a dependent clause before an independent clause.	After the concert, a crowd surrounded the tour bus.
	Use to separate two independent clauses.	The power went out during the storm, and the basement filled with water.
Colon	Use before a list.	I need the following herbs for the sauce: oregano, basil, and garlic.
	Use before a statement or quotation.	His success came down to one thing: hard work.
	Do not use a colon following a verb.	*Incorrect*: I need: pens, markers, and notebooks. *Correct*: I need these supplies for school: pens, markers, and notebooks. *(continued)*

Semicolon	Use semicolons when you have two independent clauses that are related and need a slight pause to separate them. Use semicolons before the following adverbs that separate independent clauses: however, then, indeed, accordingly, therefore, then, thus, besides, hence.	You need spaghetti, sauce, and meatballs for dinner; *don't forget the garlic bread!* My best friends live far away; however, I try to see them every year. Note: Using a semicolon is somewhat subjective, but the phrase after the semicolon must be a complete thought.
Commas versus Semicolons	Use a semicolon after items in a list that already includes commas.	My entire family attended the reunion: Aunt Vern, who brought her schnauzer, Huggy; Cousin Zelda and her children, Sissy, Suzi, and Zoe; and Uncle Herman and Aunt Erma, who live in Des Moines. *(continued)*

Direct Object	The thing that receives the action	Note: If you're unsure what the direct object is, take the verb and then ask "what?" For example: Pass the *milk* to Karla. Pass what? Pass milk. Give the *message* to Taylor. Give what? Give the message.
Indirect Object	The person or thing for whom an action is performed	Note: If you're unsure what the indirect object is, ask *to whom* something is given. For example: Pass the milk to *Karla*. Pass the milk to whom? Pass the milk to Karla. Give the message to *Taylor*. Give the message to whom? Give the message to Taylor. *(continued)*

Quotation Marks	Exact wording from a reference requires quotation marks. Keep periods and commas inside the quotation marks.	"I'll be back." (Terminator)
References	Additional sources that you use to back up your thesis Make titles of books and magazines italicized, but put articles in quotation marks.	*The Lord of the Rings: The Fellowship of the Ring* *Sports Illustrated* "On a High Note: Why Children Who Study Music Achieve Higher Grades"

7. PASSIVE VOICE

Ever notice that green squiggly line on the screen when you're typing? That line often indicates the passive voice. This topic is one of the most confusing and difficult points of grammar that you will confront, and I want to go into a detailed explanation of this concept. The passive voice harms more papers than it helps. This construction occurs when the subject of the sentence doesn't do the action; to put it another way, the word that should receive the action (the direct object) becomes the subject. Not only does the construction lose power and clarity, but the sentence also drags on with the extra words required to express the thought.

> *For example:*
> The dog is chased by the cat.   *Longer, weak*
> The cat chases the dog.   *Shorter, powerful*

In the first sentence, the subject (the dog) is not doing the chasing (the verb). He is being chased by the cat.

In the second sentence, the cat (subject) chases (verb) the dog (direct object). This sentence gets to the point more quickly and the reader is less likely to be confused.

Here's the formula for the passive voice:

> "to be" verb + a past tense verb (verb ending in -ed, -en, or -t) = passive

Sometimes, however, you may need to use the passive voice (for example, when you don't know who did the action).

> *For example:*
> It was reported that there were three people injured in the plane crash.

Evidently, the person or agency that reported this fact is unknown.

> *You could say this instead:*
> Someone reported that there were three people injured in the plane crash.

Now you have the active voice, but you're using an ambiguous pronoun. (I'll discuss this issue later.)

The best choice would be to know who did the

action (in this case, "reported") and to use the active voice whenever possible. The following words are helping verbs (they help the main verb), and they often introduce the passive voice:

am	is	are
was	were	do
did	shall	has
have	had	will
may	could	should
would	can	might
be	been	must
being	does	

The shortest and clearest way to express a thought is to put the subject of the sentence first followed by the action it's doing. Use the active voice whenever possible.

8. PROOFREAD!

Have you ever said something and immediately wished you could take it back? Proofreading allows you that opportunity in your written work.

Take the time to read and reread your paper. You won't discover an oversight unless you check your work carefully. Every writer has misspelled a word or left it out altogether, and you will kick yourself if your intelligent scribblings lose points because of your lack of diligence in this area. Even spell-check won't save you because it can neither find the mistakes in usage (for example, "to" versus "too"), nor can it tell you that you've just forgotten a letter (for example, "tap" versus "tape") or misspelled a word by hitting the wrong key (for example, "turn" versus "torn"). I recommend reading aloud because you will hear problems in a paper that you would never notice if you read it silently.

In addition, ask someone else to read it to you because that person will also notice sentences that don't make sense or don't flow from one paragraph to another. If a statement sounds awkward, you need to rework it. You already know what you're trying to say, but someone else won't unless you write clearly. You are so familiar with your subject that your eye passes over the words, and you start to see content that's not really on the page. When I've edited papers in the past, the writer has made mental leaps that the uninformed reader couldn't follow. Other people will notice your lack of clarity, and if they can't understand your paper, then you need to keep working on it.

As easy as it may be to whip off an average grade paper, make the effort to work through these steps. Remember: ovens, not microwaves.

9. SAME PERSON/SAME TENSE

Even in proofreading, you can miss certain rules if you're not aware of them. This section includes a couple rules that are often broken in the spoken language, but which you must follow in the written word.

Using the Same Person

As I discussed in "Correct Grammar and Punctuation," sentences comprise subjects and verbs. The subject and the verb must be the same ("agree") in terms of using singular and plural forms ("person and number"). That is, the singular noun must have a singular verb, and plural nouns must use plural verbs.

One of the most common mistakes occurs when a writer uses the third person singular with the third person plural:

For example:
Incorrect: A person should keep their opinion to themselves.

"person" (singular)   "their" and "themselves" (plural)

Correct: A person should keep his opinion to himself.

"person" (singular)   "his" and "himself" (singular)

or

People should keep their opinions to themselves.

Note: Although people use "themselves" in conversation and in advertising instead of the singular form to be politically correct, it's incorrect to use it in academic writing. If you use the plural form of words, you won't have to worry about sounding sexist by using the singular.

	Singular Verb	*Plural Verb*
1st Person	I am	We are
2nd Person	You are	You are
3rd Person	He is	They are

A complicated and lengthy sentence (using many phrases that separate the subject and the verb) can cause the writer to lose track of the subject and choose the incorrect form of the verb, so keep it short!

For example:
The exam and final term paper, due to the extenu-
ating circumstances of stormy weather, crashing
computers, and a stolen copy of the test, has been
delayed, which excited the class tremendously.

The sentence went on and on, so the writer acci-
dentally used the incorrect form of the verb. "Exam
and final term paper" were the subjects of the sentence.
The verb should have been plural ("have") to agree
with the two subjects, but because of the length of the
sentence, the writer inevitably made it singular.

Corrected example:
The exam and final term paper, due to the extenu-
ating circumstances of stormy weather, crashing
computers, and a stolen copy of the test, have been
delayed, which excited the class tremendously,
and there was a resounding cheer heard for miles
around.

Perhaps you were wondering if you could use
"were" instead of "have been" in the previous example.
The answer is no, if you want to retain the original
meaning. Why? Let's talk about tenses.

Tenses

A tense is the time in which an event occurs in your writing. There are various "times" indicated by the verb form.

> *For example:*
> I am writing.   *Present tense*
> I wrote.   *Past tense*
> I will write.   *Future tense*

You may not realize it, but you write in the past, present, and future times most often. You will probably choose past or present for the majority of the work, but you must stay in the same tense (or time) once you choose. It's confusing for the reader to jump back and forth.

> *For example:*
> **Incorrect:** Benjamin Franklin wrote Poor Richard's Almanac and says, "A penny saved is a penny earned."
>
> **Correct:**   Benjamin Franklin wrote Poor Richard's Almanac and said, "A penny saved is a penny earned."
>
> *Remember:* stay in the same tense throughout your writing, or you may confuse your reader.

10. AMBIGUOUS PRONOUNS

> "I was talking to a friend, and he was telling me about his friend and how he went to the game at the stadium. He told me he had a lot of fun at it."

Have you ever had a conversation like this? Were you confused? Who had fun? Who enjoyed the game or the stadium? You have just discovered the danger of ambiguous pronouns.

Choose specific, "concrete" words in your writing. Authors often lose their readers when they use pronouns instead of particular nouns.

For example:
Someone somewhere should do something about this.

This sentence is a rather extreme case, but you get the point. The following words don't give you specific information:

anything	nothing	something
it	all	some
they	what	no one
this	that	

Look at Example 1 again and then look at Example 2 with concrete nouns.

Example 1:
Someone somewhere should do something about this.

Example 2:
The citizens of this town should organize a food drive to help the destitute families.

Concrete nouns clear up any confusion. Take the time to choose a concrete noun; this is better than taking the easy road and using a pronoun. Your writing can lose power if you use an ambiguous pronoun when a specific noun would make your point clearer and prove that you know what you're talking about. This section goes hand in hand with the chapter on vocabulary. Pronouns aren't necessarily bad; they do have their place (like here). Just make sure the reader won't misunderstand your meaning by using too many pronouns.

Reference Tables

The following tables include commonly misused and misunderstood words and phrases:

Irregular Verb Forms—verbs people often have problems with in the past tense

Irregular Adjectival Forms—adjectives that have "odd" endings when compared and those that you can't compare

Troublesome Words—seemingly similar words that have specific usage (including examples)

Problematic Pronouns and Their Usage—pronouns with a description of their usage (including examples)

Problematic Phrases and Their Usage—phrases and constructions that people use or form incorrectly, with a description of their usage (including examples)

Possessives—descriptions and examples to help you choose the correct form

Latin Expressions—meanings and correct usage of three common expressions

The final table, *Transitional Words*, provides examples to help your paper flow smoothly from one idea to the next.

Irregular Verb Forms

Present Tense	Past Tense	Past Participle†
Bring	Brought	Brought
Eat	Ate	Eaten
Drink	Drank	Drunk
Drive	Drove	Driven
Give	Gave	Given
Go	Went	Gone
Hang (Object)	Hung	Hung
Hanged (Person)	Hanged	Hanged
Lie (Person)	Lay	Lain *(continued)*

Lay (Object)	Laid	Laid
Swim	Swam	Swum
Write	Wrote	Written

† *These verb forms are always preceded by some combination of the following helping verbs: am, is, are, was, were, do, did, shall, has, have, had, will, may, could, should, would, can, might, be, been, must, being, and does.*

Irregular Adjectival Forms

Adjective	Comparative Form (of two)	Superlative Form (of at least three)
Bad	Worse	Worst
Good	Better	Best
Equal	Incomparable Adjective It doesn't have degrees of equality. It's incorrect to say that something is very equal or more equal. It either is or it isn't.	

(continued)

Dominant	Incomparable Adjective It doesn't have degrees of dominance. It's incorrect to say that something is very dominant or more dominant. It either is or it isn't.
Unique	Incomparable Adjective It doesn't have degrees of uniqueness. It's incorrect to say that something is very unique or more unique. It either is or it isn't.
Complete	Incomparable Adjective It doesn't have degrees of completeness. It's incorrect to say that something is very complete or more complete. It either is or it isn't.
Favorite	Incomparable Adjective It doesn't have degrees of being a favorite. It's incorrect to say that something is very favorite or more favorite. It either is or it isn't.
Perfect	Incomparable Adjective It doesn't have degrees of being perfect. It's incorrect to say that something is very perfect or more perfect. It either is or it isn't.

(continued)

Superior	Incomparable Adjective It doesn't have degrees of being superior. It's incorrect to say that something is very superior or more superior. It either is or it isn't.

Troublesome Words

Word	Usage	Example
Number	When you can count a quantity	The plane only has a certain *number* of seats available. (You can count the number of "seats.") But: There's a limited *amount* of space on the plane. (You can't quantify "space.")
Amount	When you can't count a quantity	Jenny guessed the *amount* of money in that jar. But: Maria guessed the *number* of pennies in that jar. *(continued)*

Fewer	Comparing a quantity that you can count	That cashier takes ten items or *fewer*. (You can count the number of "items.") But: That cashier takes people with *less* stuff in their carts.
Less	Comparing a quantity that you can't count	There's less snow on the ground today than yesterday. (You can't quantify the noun "snow.") But: There are fewer inches of snow today than yesterday.
While*	During an interval of time	While we drove cross-country, Antonio talked incessantly.
Whereas	While on the contrary Use when you're comparing dissimilar things.	Michael likes raisins whereas Christine prefers chocolate. *(continued)*

Good	Adjective—modifies a noun or pronoun	The good weather continued all weekend. I feel good. ("Good" modifies "I." It refers to my state of mind.) Never say "It's going good." Only say "I'm doing good" if you mean that you're bringing about a positive effect in a situation.
Well*	Adverb—modifies a verb, an adjective, or another adverb	Now that it's fixed, the car runs very well. I feel well. ("Well" modifies "feel.")
Farther	Greater distance (comparative form of the word far)	Kenny was farther from the campsite than he thought. *(continued)*

Further	To a more advanced degree or in more detail Note: Although "farther" and "further" have been used interchangeably to mean distance, now "further" is more often used solely as "extent" or "addition."	When you have more time, let's discuss this issue further.
Comprise	Use when you refer to the whole that is made up of numerous parts	The university comprises many buildings.
Compose	Use when you refer to the parts that make up the whole	Many buildings compose the university.
Take*	Carry something away (from the speaker) The person being addressed is physically moving away from the speaker.	*Take* your jacket with you to school!
Bring*	Carry something	*Bring* me the newspaper. We're *bringing* dessert with us. *(continued)*

Infer	Conclude after hearing or reading something	From her tone of voice, Craig *inferred* that his mother disapproved of his plan.
Imply	Suggest without directly saying	Angie's rude behavior to Melissa *implied* that they were no longer friends.
Assure‡	Removes doubt	Let me *assure* you that there are no monsters under your bed.
Ensure‡	Implies guarantee	Sprinkler systems *ensure* that fires will remain contained.
Insure‡	Stresses taking precautions	*Insure* your safety by keeping a fire extinguisher in your kitchen and fresh batteries in your smoke detector. *(continued)*

Between†	Involving two people or things	Just *between* you and me, I'm going to surprise my husband with a trip to Cabo San Lucas. *Note:* Never say "between you and I." Split the candy bar *between* the two of you.
Among†	Involving more than two people or things	*Among* my neighbors, the Poulins have the nicest lawn.
Effect	Noun—end result Verb—to produce a result	Exercise had a great *effect* on the injured horse. Charlene can *effect* change as a member of the council.
Affect	Noun—feeling or emotion As a general rule, don't use the noun except in the field of psychology. Verb—to cause or to fake a characteristic that isn't truly part of a person's personality	The criminal had a flat *affect*. The flu *affected* the whole school. Mike Myers makes us all laugh when he *affects* funny accents. *(continued)*

Moot	Something that's not worth debating	Considering that the game is over, the fact that the call was wrong is a *moot* point.
Mute	Adjective—Unable (or possibly unwilling) to speak Noun—someone who can't speak	Helen Keller was deaf and *mute*. The young *mute* was an excellent confidante, as he could tell no secrets.
Revert	Never follow with the word "back." It's redundant. "Revert" already means "to go back."	In the presence of his childhood pals, Eric *reverted* to adolescence.
Accept*	To receive or to agree	Julia *accepted* the bad news quietly. Liam *accepted* the offer on his car.
Except*	Excluding	The class ran outside, *except* Josh, who sat sullenly at his desk.

* *These words can function as multiple parts of speech or have numerous definitions. I'm trying to focus on the most problematic constructions, so I'm not describing every use of a particular word. To find more information, use a large dictionary that has extensive entries.*

† *Some sources say it's acceptable to use both words depending on whether the relationship stresses distribution or individuals.*

‡ *In most contexts, these words are synonymous.*

Problematic Pronouns and Their Usage

Word	Part of Speech	Example
I	Pronoun (Subject)	*I* walked to the store. *We* attended a concert last night. *He* and Matt work together. *They* and Michelle studied for the exam.
We		
She/He		
They		
		(continued)

Me	Pronoun (Indirect and Direct Object) Note: *Do not begin sentences with these words.*	Send (to) *me* the report before 5 p.m. (Indirect Object) Talk to *us* later about the job. (Indirect Object) Joanne saw *him/her/them* last night. (Saw whom? Saw him/her/them. [Direct Object])
Us		
Her/Him		
Them		
Its	Possessive Pronoun	A snake sheds *its* skin.
It's	Contraction of Pronoun and verb "It is"	*It's* too late to order pizza.
Whose*	Possessive Pronoun	*Whose* coat is lying there?
Who's	Contraction of Pronoun	*Who's* on the schedule tomorrow night?
Who	Pronoun Subject	*Who* knows the answer to the question? *She/he/they* know the answer. *(continued)*

Whom	Pronoun Direct Object	*Whom* did you call? I called him/her/them. (Called whom? Called him. [Direct Object]) If it makes sense to use *him*, *her*, or *them* in a sentence, then use *whom*. Notice the "m" in *him* and the*m* and the "m" in who*m*.
	Pronoun Indirect Object	Vanessa gave John the key. (Gave what? Gave key [Direct object] Gave to whom? Gave to John (him) [Indirect Object]
Their	Possessive Pronoun	The police officer ticketed *their* car.
There*	Adverb	*There* are my dogs Conan and Cosmo.
They're	Pronoun Contraction of Pronoun and verb "They are"	*They're* friends of ours.

(continued) |

What*	Pronoun Takes the place of the subject	*What* is your favorite book? *What* is the name of Harry's lizard?
Which*	Adjective Modifies the subject	*Which* color do you prefer? *Which* player scored the touchdown?

* *These words can function as multiple parts of speech. I'm trying to focus on the most problematic constructions, so I'm not describing every use of a particular word. To find more information, use a large dictionary that has extensive entries.*

Problematic Phrases and Their Usage

Phrase	Usage	Example
Feel bad	Adjective ("bad") that modifies the subject Adjectives describe nouns.	Anna *feels bad* about her disagreement with Karen. "Bad" describes Anna, not "feels." *(continued)*

Feel badly	Adverb ("badly") modifies the verb (feel) Adverbs modify other adverbs and verbs.	Correct: After the accident, I *feel badly* with my left hand. Literally, the limb doesn't sense objects well. Incorrect: I feel badly about causing the accident. This example is incorrect, because "badly" describes "feel" and not "I."
Different from	Never say "different than."	The houses were only *different from* each other in terms of color.
Combined Ownership	Two people (or more) own one thing, make the second (or last) name possessive	*Eileen and Marc's* house *Peter, Tommy, and Jack's* toys
Separate Ownership	Two or more people own separate items	*Tim's and Robert's* cars

(continued)

I wish I were... If I were you...	Subjunctive mood These are examples of situations that are contrary to fact. They aren't real, which is why you use "were" instead of the present tense of the verb to be ("was").	If Chris *were* a millionaire, he would sail around the world. Wish you *were* here! *Were* Alison shorter, she would've become a jockey.
Try to	When it's followed by a verb, "Try" always takes the infinitive. Never say "try and."	*Try to* be on time. The detectives *try to* find the criminal. ("To be" and "to find" are the infinitive forms of the verbs.)

Possessives

Singular Noun	Loretta	Loretta's
Singular Noun Ending in s	Charles	Charles' or Charles's *(continued)*

Plural Noun	Children Men	Children's Men's
Plural Noun Ending in s	Monkeys Houses	Monkeys' Houses'
Singular Noun with Multiple Members	Smith (family)	the Smiths' house

Latin Expressions

Latin	Meaning	Correct Usage
i.e.	that is Explaining an idea in more depth	Dew Point is the temperature at which water vapor reaches the saturation point (*i.e.*, 100% humidity).
e.g.	for example Giving an example of an idea	Make sure you take the essentials for your hike (*e.g.*, food, sunscreen, hat, and extra water). *(continued)*

etc.	and others Telling the reader there are more unspecified details like the ones already mentioned	A homeowner needs tools like a hammer, screw driver, wrench, *etc.*

Transitional Words

To	Use These Words:
Present Results	therefore, as a result, consequently
Present New Ideas/Claims/ Information, etc.	moreover, furthermore, in addition, likewise
Define/Clarify Support	for example, for instance, in other words
Contrast Ideas	however, on the contrary, on the other hand, rather
Reinforce Ideas	further, in particular, indeed, above all
Summarize	thus, in conclusion